IAN PLIMER

THE LITTLE GREEN BOOK TWO

FOR TEENS

Austrotengella plimeri – a Spider ... and Plimerite – the Mineral

PROFESSOR
IAN PLIMER

PROFESSOR IAN PLIMER is Australia's best-known geologist. He is Emeritus Professor of Earth Sciences at the University of Melbourne, where he was Professor and Head of Earth Sciences. He was Professor at the University of Newcastle, Professor at The University of Adelaide and Professor in Munich (Germany). He was also on the staff at the University of New England, the University of New South Wales, Macquarie University and North Broken Hill Ltd.

He has published more than 130 scientific papers on geology and was an editor of the *Encyclopedia of Geology*. This is his thirteenth book written for the general public. Professor Plimer has received numerous national and international awards for his scientific work.

A new Broken Hill mineral, plimerite, was named in recognition of his contribution to Broken Hill geology. A ground-hunting rainforest spider *Austrotengella plimeri* from the Tweed Range (NSW) has been named in his honour.

Published in 2023 by Connor Court Publishing Pty Ltd
Copyright © Ian Plimer

All rights reserved. No part of this book may be reproduced or transmitted in any form or by any means, electronic or mechanical, including photocopying, recording or by any information storage and retrieval system, without prior permission in writing from the publisher.

Connor Court Publishing Pty Ltd
PO Box 7257
Redland Bay QLD 4165
sales@connorcourt.com
www.connorcourtpublishing.com.au

ISBN: 9781922815668
Front Cover: JGD Design and Web, Melbourne.
Printed in Australia

I find it frustrating, as a lay person, to find answers to technical questions. You see gigantic wind turbines appearing all over the country, but there is very little about the practical value of these monstrosities ... When will common sense and good science prevail and what happens if it does not fairly soon?

Letter from HRH Prince Philip to Professor Plimer, 29th April 2018.

—

This book attempts to answer the questions raised by the late Duke of Edinburgh.

A planet in crisis?

> *UNCOMFORTABLE TRUTH:*
> *No one has ever shown that human emissions of carbon dioxide drive global warming. If it was shown, then it would also have to be shown that the natural emissions, 97% of the total, don't drive global warming. This also has not been done.*

We are told that increasing emissions of carbon dioxide by humans will lead to a climate crisis and increased hurricanes, flooding, fires, droughts, hot weather, starvation, melting of ice sheets, destruction of the Great Barrier Reef, sea level rise and all sorts of other scary things.

Measurements shows that this is not true. Whatever you might feel or think, changes to the planet can be measured.

> *BURY THE TRUTH: Hidden in Chapter 11 of the UN's IPCC AR6 climate report is a table that shows there is no increase in severe weather events. Why don't we hear this in the mainstream media that tells us we have a climate crisis? Maybe it's because disaster sells, good news does not. I don't trust the media. Do you?*

Are more people being killed by climate disasters as humans put more carbon dioxide into the air? No.

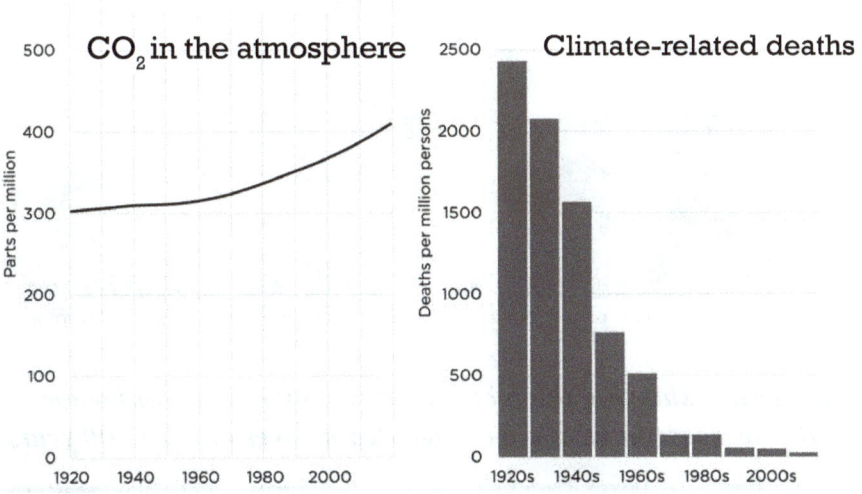

Diagrams showing the increase in carbon dioxide in the air and the decrease in weather-related deaths over the last 100 years.

Storms can kill people. In wealthy countries, buildings are stronger and can survive storms far better than in poor countries. This means fewer people get killed.

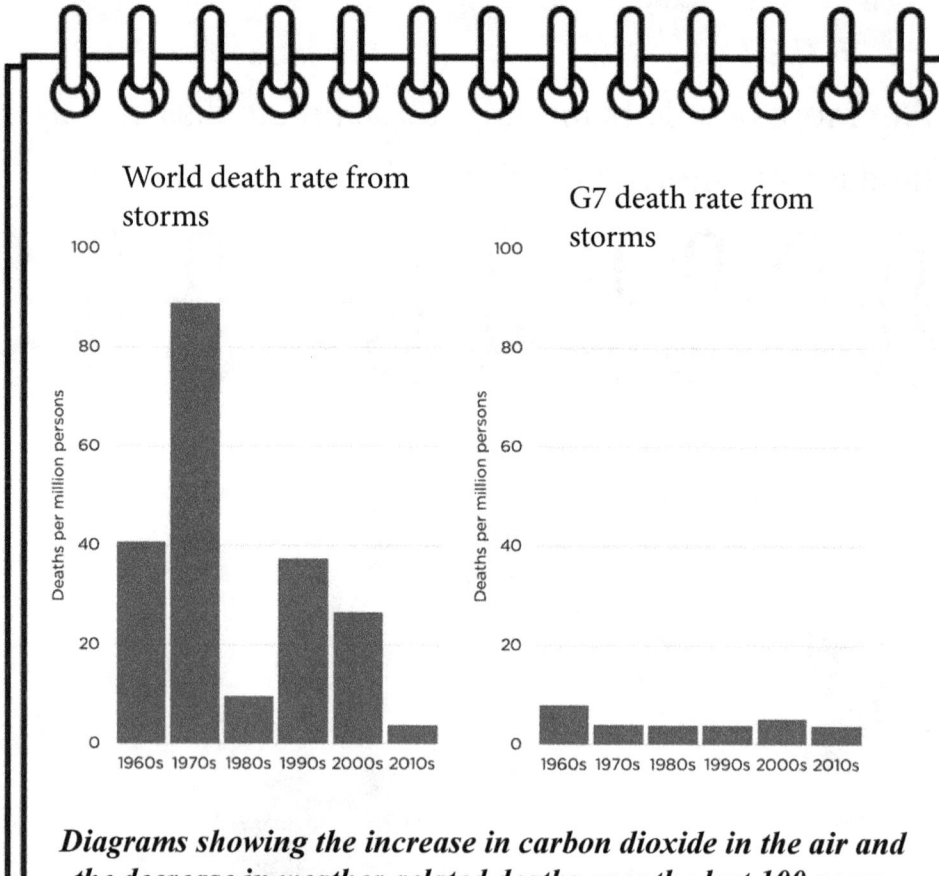

Diagrams showing the increase in carbon dioxide in the air and the decrease in weather-related deaths over the last 100 years.

The cost of damaging storms, hurricanes, cyclones, floods and fires varies from year-to-year. It has not increased over the last 40 years due to increased emissions of carbon dioxide by humans.

We are told that increasing carbon dioxide in the air will produce more hurricanes. In the US, Florida is the state that gets hit by hurricanes the most. If human emissions of carbon dioxide are increasing, then the number of hurricanes should also be increasing. They are not.

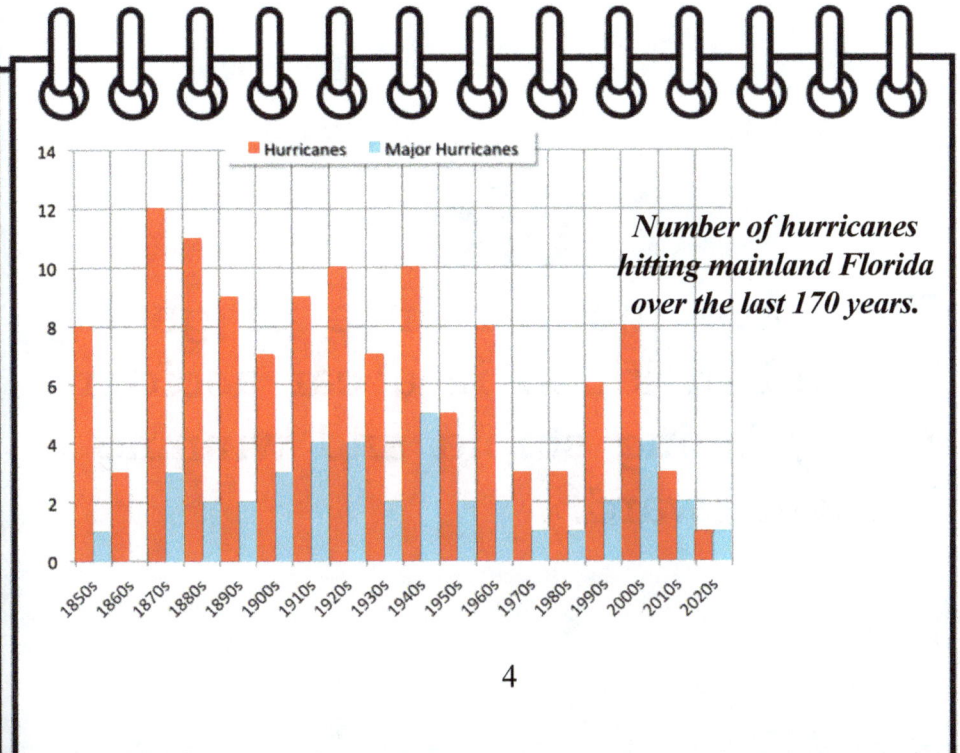

Number of hurricanes hitting mainland Florida over the last 170 years.

> CYCLONES: Cyclones kill coral and smash up the Great Barrier Reef. Sand from the smashed reef forms most of the sediment around the reef, there is almost no sediment from the land and chemicals used in farming many kilometres landward of the Reef have not been detected in water or sediment.

Are we really going to fry and die in a climate crisis or get smashed up in a hurricane?

Is there a climate emergency?

No.

You have more chance of getting injured or killed in a car accident. Or by being stupid and winning a Darwin Award.

***Global Burned Area
(normalised)***

The world is becoming a better place. The area burned each year is getting less. Headline news pictures from a terrible massive wildfire somewhere on the planet don't tell you what is happening on the whole planet.

The Sahara is hot, windy and dry. There are no forest fires because there is no fuel to burn. There are catastrophic fires in temperate forests because of the build-up of fuel and explosive chemicals in leaves. Fires have nothing to do with climate and everything to do with the amount of fuel left lying around.

A major source of air pollution is smoke from forest fires. For example, smoke from fires in western Canada in 2023 covered Norway. Smoke from the 2020 forest fires in eastern Australia was seen and smelled in New Zealand.

Most forests are state owned and suffer from a lack of

maintenance. Pressure from environmental groups has reduced low temperature winter burning of small areas to reduce the fuel load. The fuel load builds up after long periods of rain and without regular fires.

Humans have been preventing wildfires for tens of thousands of years in Africa, Canada and Australia by regular small low temperature winter burns.

Most forest and grass fires are started by humans, especially on hot windy days after a long dry time. **About 75% of fires are lit by arsonists** with many others started from sparks from machinery and power lines. Lightning starts some wildfires.

People living in and around forests get cooked in large wildfires, as do native animals and trees. The environmental damage from one huge wildfire is far greater than the damage from numerous

Own the fuel, own the fire

controlled small low temperature winter fires.

If forests are locked up for environment protection and not managed, one day they will be destroyed by a catastrophic fire that kills everything. This is not environmentalism.

If you don't want catastrophic wildfires, put local foresters in charge of the forests. Foresters care for the next generation of trees and people, use local knowledge and don't sit hundreds of kilometres from the front line.

Timber is just another recyclable resource. It just takes longer to grow from a seedling to a tree compared with wheat. In Finland, each generation of farmers gets one cut of timber from their forest, they re-plant and the re-planted forest is later harvested by their children.

This forest management is far better for the environment compared to many other countries that use illegal timber stolen from forests.

Sometimes there is very heavy rain, other times there is drought. There are many reasons for this, the normal reasons being the El Niño-La Niña cycle in the Pacific Ocean or changing ocean currents.

Climate activists shout that every slight change, be it a dust storm, heavy rain or broken fingernails, is a result of climate change. Maybe there are other natural processes that people don't think about.

One reason for very heavy rain periods that does not get raised in the mainstream media are rain bombs resulting from volcanoes. After the Calbuco volcano erupted in Chile on 7th January 1893, Brisbane had the biggest rain bomb and the biggest floods ever recorded in February 1893.

In 2011, volcanic ash from the Chilean volcano Puyehue-Cordon-Caulle shut Sydney airport for a week. It then travelled around the world again and shut down airports 10 days later.

After the Hunga Tonga eruption in Tonga in 2022, unusually heavy rain fell over Australia. After the volcanic dust had gone for another lap around the world, there were more rain bombs and glorious sunsets in Australia.

Volcanic eruptions have changed civilisations, such as the Thira eruption in about 1600 BC. This led to the collapse of the Minoan empire.

It's happened before and will happen again. An explosive supervolcano eruption will be a catastrophic event for the planet. Previous supervolcano eruptions have led to collapses in civilisation, famine, disease, war, global cooling, excessive rain and mass deaths. Demand your government make laws to stop future supervolcano eruptions. They will be as useful as laws made to stop climate change.

After the 1783-1784 AD eruptions of Laki in Iceland, there were choking clouds of sulphur gases over Europe. People died of lung failure, crops died, there was heavy rain, famine and the average temperature dropped 5 degrees.

After the April 1815 eruption of Tambora in Indonesia, 1816 became known as the year without the summer. It was grey, cold and wet.

After the 1883 Krakotoa (Indonesia) and 1991 Pinatubo (Philippines), there were also cool summers and heavy rain.

One volcano can ruin your whole day. History shows us that volcanic eruptions change the course of history, weather and climate.

Be very careful when you hear the word **"unprecedented"**. This means that the person making the claim ignores history. The 2023 floods at Loxton on the Murray River (Australia) were claimed to be **unprecedented.**

However, the "tree of knowledge" at Loxton has markers showing the maximum height of previous floods. The biggest flood on record was in 1956. The 2023 flood was not **unprecedented.** You were fed BS by the media.

In eastern Australia and California, heavy rains are often followed the following summer by huge wildfires.

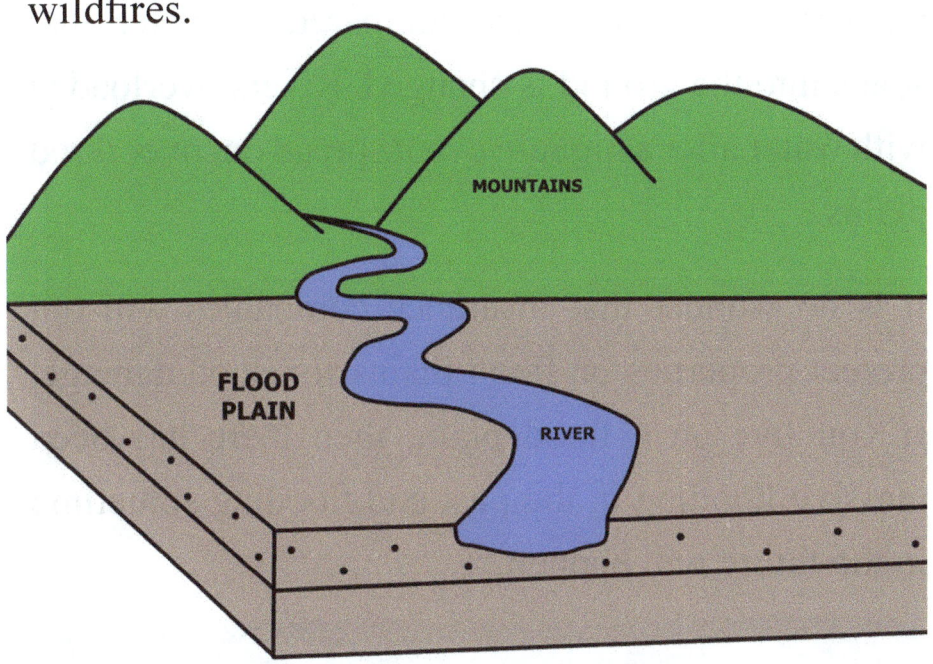

Watercourses change from high energy streams in mountains to large low energy meandering rivers closer to the sea that constantly change their course. Flood plains occur because of the build-up of sediment after countless events of flooding by big rivers over millions of years.

By building houses and roads on flood plains, the amount of run-off water compared to water that soaks into the ground is changed. Rivers overloaded with water after a big rain event spread out over flood plains.

It is no wonder that insurance companies will not protect properties on flood plains for flood damage. If you live on a flood plain, then there has been massive flooding in the past and flooding sometime in the future will happen.

> **DUMB QUESTION:**
> *Are flood plains called flood plains because there are frequent floods?*

If you can't measure it, then it does not exist.

In Central Park, New York, the temperature has been measured for nearly 150 years. Can you see a temperature rise due to humans emitting an increased amount of carbon dioxide over the last 40, 80 or even 120 years? **No.**

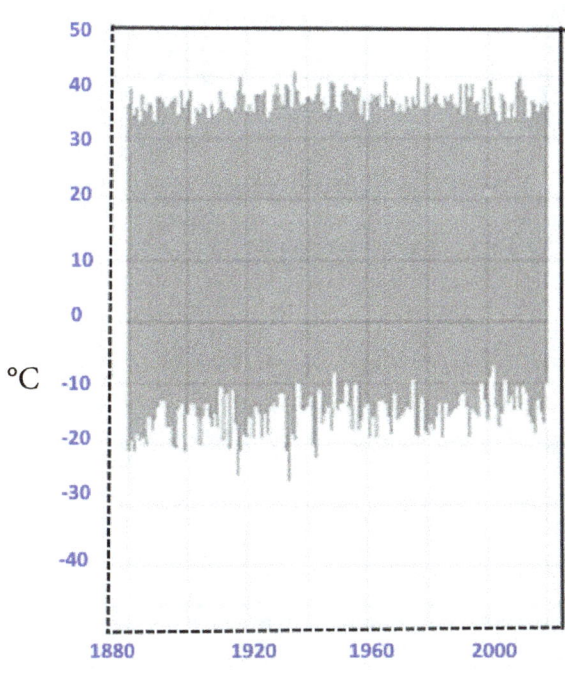

The 150-year temperature record in Central Park, New York.

Are people in the US or Australia cooking because of a climate emergency?

No.

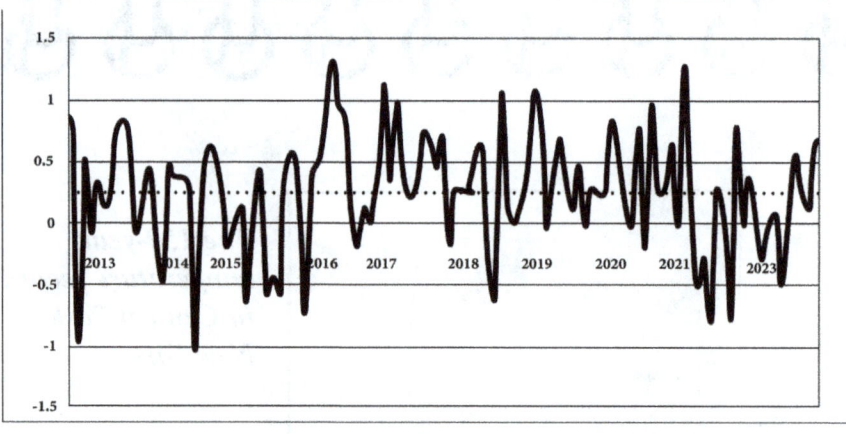

The temperature record in Australian from 1991 until 2020. There is no warming trend. I'm sick of waiting to fry and die in a climate emergency. I want to get on with life.

Now tell me again. Are we in a climate crisis or climate emergency? Maybe people have worked out a way to make a lot of money by scaring us about a mythical climate crisis and telling us that we will fry and die because we are all scared of dying.

Cries of a climate crisis and climate emergency are, at best, a massive exaggeration. It may well be disinformation and a mechanism to control every aspect of our lives.

Do you really want to eat bugs, travel less, walk to school and have no electricity as a method of changing climate?

DID YOU KNOW?
Urban areas with trees have fewer deaths in hot weather than those with just concrete and bricks. The temperature in cities is 1.5°C warmer than in the countryside. Wherever you live, plant trees.**

**(For parents/grandparents: Other studies show that green spaces reduce cardiovascular disease, dementia and poor metal health and improve the cognitive functioning of children and the elderly).

An increase in carbon dioxide in the air does not lead to an increase in temperature. The US and the rest of the world show a very slight temperature decrease despite the carbon dioxide in air increasing. This shows carbon dioxide cannot drive climate change.

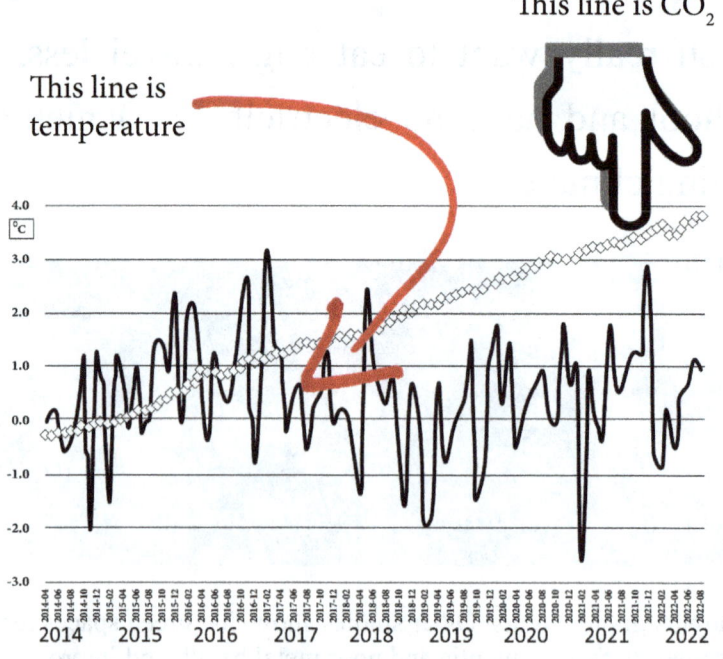

Sometimes summers are hotter than those you remember. Other times summers are cooler. During the time you have been alive, there has been no measured global warming. There have been the odd hot days. So what? The trend is your friend.

However, there has been a lot of hot air from activists trying to make themselves sound important by frightening you. They claim you will fry and die and that it's your fault.

> *DID YOU KNOW?*
> *There are five major climate zones: polar, dry, moist sub-tropical mid-latitude, moist continental mid-latitude and tropical. The US has at least 6 climate zones, as does Australia. The UK has one.*

Humans have adapted to live in all climate zones on our planet. A warmer, wetter, colder or drier climate does not kill us. We adapt and have done so for a very long time as we have always lived with climate change. At present, humans live in tropical, temperate, desert, mountainous and polar regions. Maybe in your lifetime, humans will live in space and in the deep oceans.

> **THE PERFECT CLIMATE:**
> *Dayaks living in the jungles of Borneo would claim they live in a perfect climate. So would the Bedouins in the deserts of the Middle East, the tribal Australian aboriginals or the Sami people of polar Lapland. They all have adapted to extreme climates. What is the perfect climate for you?*

If an increased carbon dioxide content in the air drives global warming, then we should be warming. We are not. You are being told nonsense.

When snow falls, it traps small amounts of air that remains trapped when the snow is compressed to ice. From chemical fingerprints in the ice and trapped air, we know that thousands of years after a natural warming event, the carbon dioxide content of the air increased. This is the exact opposite of the scary story that claims that carbon dioxide drives the temperature of air.

Ice has only been on Earth for 20% of time. For 80% of time, the Earth has been warmer and wetter than now and with a higher sea level. The Earth is presently in an ice age.

Glaciation is when the ice grows and an interglacial is when the ice shrinks. Interglacials last about 10,000 years, our modern interglacial started about 14,700 years ago.

Ice that covered Europe, England, Canada and Russia melted as the planet warmed. This gave a sea level rise of 130 metres. After some past ice ages, sea level rose at least 600 metres.

Sea level rose and plants spread towards the poles and to higher altitudes as the temperature and rainfall increased. During glaciation, there were land bridges across areas that are now water.

People and animals migrated across these land bridges. People walked from Russia to Alaska, from Europe to England, from Papua New Guinea to Australia and from mainland Australia to Tasmania.

> *We were at the highest interglacial temperature 7,000 to 4,000 years ago. We have been cooling for the last 4,000 years in a longer-term cooling trend with periods of warming and cooling.*

Over the last 4,000 years of cooling, the warm periods led to the rise of great empires. There was extra and better food, people were healthier and lived longer and there was more money. In cold times there was crop failure, starvation, disease, more wars and people died young.

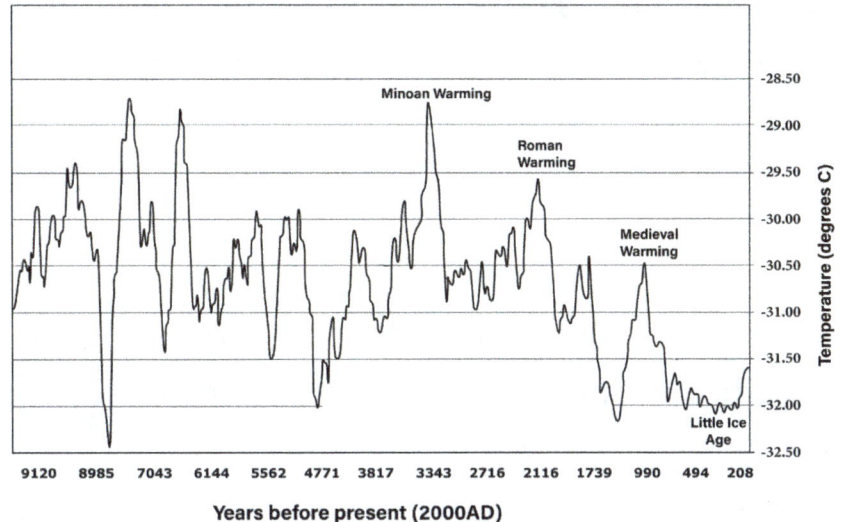

The Greenland temperature record from ice cores showing the peak of the current interglacial 7,000 to 4,000 years ago and long-term cooling with warm and cool times.

TRICK QUESTION

If you are ever asked whether the planet is warming or cooling, the only correct answer is "Yes".

you are told the planet is warming, your reply must be "Since when?" The planet has been cooling since Minoan times. It also cooled since Roman times.

Do you think there would be warming or cooling after the Little Ice Age?

There was no fossil fuel burning in Minoan, Roman and Medieval times yet it was warmer than today. Why?

HINT: Maybe natural cycles of heating and cooling are far more important than emissions from the burning of fossil fuels which we are told changes climate.

It is claimed that there has been human-induced warming since the Industrial Revolution in the early 1800s. Of course. The early 1800s was in the Little Ice Age.

During cold times in the Little Ice Age, crops failed, there was starvation and disease. Natural cycles of climate were not understood and, of course, someone had to be blamed. Many women were killed during the coldest times of the Little Ice Age because it was thought that witches caused the crop failures.

This is a good example of emotion with no evidence. The emotional hysteria of human-induced climate change today is no different.

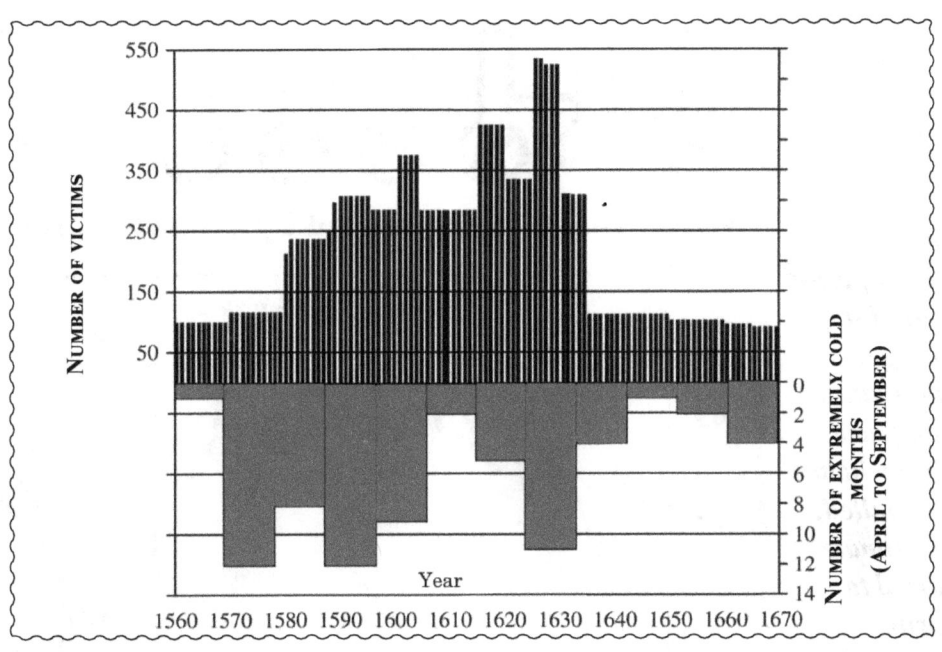

Witch killing took place when there had been a large number of extremely cold months.

After the killing of witches in the coldest period of the Little Ice Age, the planet started to warm up. Does this mean killing witches warmed the planet?

> QUESTION: Why did the planet warm after the killing of witches?
> ANSWER: The Sun became a little more active and released more energy. The Sun has now entered a Grand Solar Minimum which solar physicists think will last from 2020 to 2053. If you are a witch, run away and hide.

During the coldest period of the Little Ice Age, witch killing took place. After witches were killed, the climate started to warm.

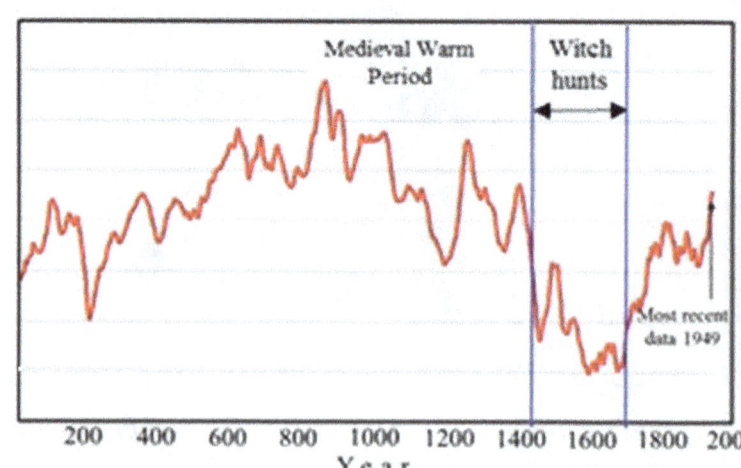

Witch hunts were fueled by climate change

Many scientists don't think that human emissions of carbon dioxide are warming the planet. These people get cancelled or go to Facebook gaol but fortunately don't suffer the same deathly fate as witches. In today's world, many people lose their jobs for thinking differently. Is that fair?

Sometimes much of the population goes nuts all at once. Killing witches because of natural climate change is one example.

Another was the **Dutch tulip craze** (1634-1637 AD) when people spent the equivalent of two years pay to buy a rare tulip bulb.

When the price of bulbs fell through the floor, a mountain of money was lost and Holland went from the richest country in the world to a poor country.

Today the Western world is going nuts about climate change while the rest of the world isn't. Western governments are spending your future by fixing a non-problem with non-solutions.

Throughout history, people have feared the cold times and thrived in warm times. Today people now fear a 2-3°C temperature rise. This is the temperature change when we move from one room to another. When we go outside the temperature change can be more than 10°C.

We love the warm weather. People go to warm climates for holidays. History and medical records show us that cold weather kills more than ten times as many people as hot weather.

WAIT FOR IT!!!

HERE COMES A HISTORY LESSON

TURN THE PAGE.....

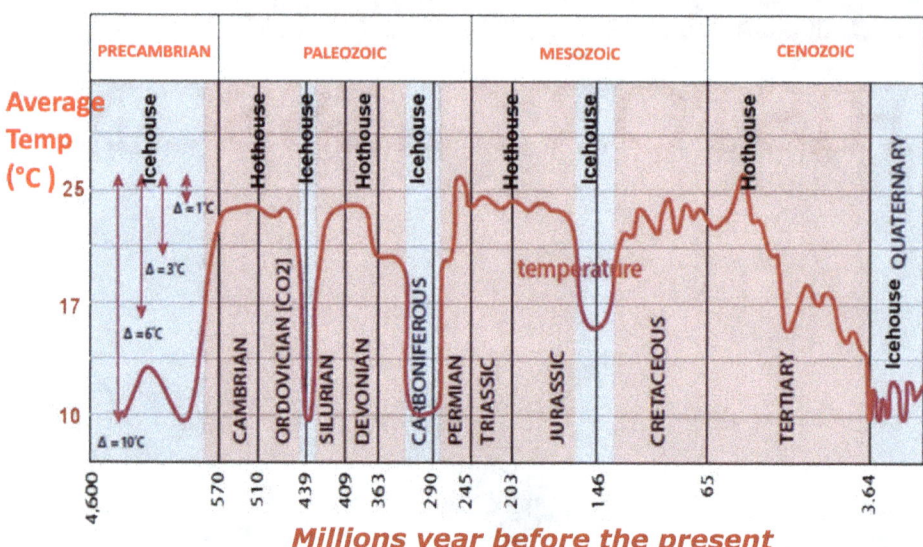

Hothouse and icehouse conditions over the last 650 million years. Earth is currently in an icehouse after 50 million years of cooling. Compared to now, for most of the last 500 million years, it has been warmer and wetter and sea level has been higher.

Over hundreds of millions of years we can see that the Earth has had many hothouse and icehouse conditions.

In icehouse conditions 650 million years ago, the planet was so cold that there were ice sheets kilometres thick at the equator and at sea level.

Do we see ice at sea level at the equator today? Obviously, natural climate changes can be fearfully large.

We are living in one of the coldest periods for hundreds of millions of years. Over the last 50 million years, we have been cooling. Ice appeared on Antarctica 34 million years ago. Greenland may have had ice off and on between 56 and 34 million years ago and the current Greenland ice sheet formed around 2.5 million years ago.

Look at the diagram. How much did temperature drop in icehouse conditions?

> *Do you really want to fear something?*
>
> **Look up the 1859 Carrington Event. If that happened today there would be no electricity, no satellites, no internet, no mobile phones, no radio and no transport. We would be blasted back 200 years in a zombie apocalypse event from which it could take decades to recover. Carrington Events occurred before 1859 when there was no modern electronic world and no systems to crash. Carrington Events will happen again.**

We are in another icehouse within which we have cooler times when the ice grows (glaciation) and warmer times (interglacial) when the ice shrinks.

QUESTION: Do you think that if the government makes new laws, then the climate will be changed from our current icehouse to a hothouse?

In today's ice age, we have short warm interglacials and long periods of glaciation. Today's interglacial is not as warm or as long as previous interglacials.

> **DID YOU KNOW?**
>
> *Two million years ago, Greenland was 10-17°C warmer than now and had elephant-like mammals, mastodon, reindeer, hares, lemmings, poplars, cedar, larch and beech. Now it has an ice cap.*

> **Drop a slice of bread with jam 100 times. Does it land jam side up or jam side down?**

During glaciation, there are huge changes in temperature, up and down. The first humans on Earth lived during glaciation and interglacials. Humans very nearly became extinct due to a supervolcano during the last glaciation about 74,000 years ago.

After this near-death event, there were only 4,000 breeding pairs of humans left on Earth. Other human species such as the Neandertals became extinct during the last glaciation.

During the last glaciation, the lowest temperature and thickest ice sheets were about 20,000 years ago. Much of northern Europe, Russia, Canada and the US were covered by kilometres of ice.

Warming was very fast and our interglacial period began 14,700 years ago. In the glaciations, there were short warmer times.

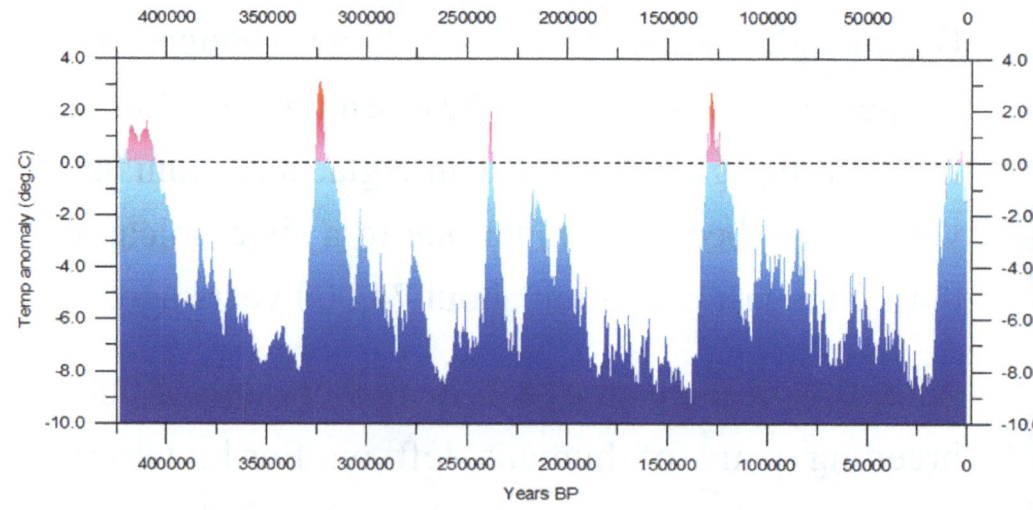

The glaciation-interglacial cycles over the last 400,000 years driven by the Earth's distance from the Sun.

In our current interglacial, the best-known cold period is called the **Younger Dryas.** It was between 12,900 and 11,600 years ago. The oceans and air cooled very quickly.

This is when humans started to live in fortified villages and grow grain rather than collect wild grain seeds in the bush. They domesticated quieter non-carnivorous animals like cattle and sheep.

Ice cores from Greenland show that there was a warming event after the Younger Dryas of at least 15°C. Humans did not die from this huge rapid global warming after the Younger Dryas. It was the opposite. They thrived.

Glaciers grow in glaciation and shrink during warm interglacials. The Little Ice Age ended in 1850 AD.

QUESTION:
Do you think that glaciers would grow or shrink after the cold Little Ice Age?

Have a look at a bubbling soft drink. The bubbles are carbon dioxide. It is colourless, does not smell and has no taste. Do you think that if carbon dioxide was a pollutant or poisonous it would be safe to drink a soft drink?

Have you ever made a cake or bread? When the cake mixture is cooked, it rises because of carbon dioxide bubbling out of the mix. These bubbles leave many little holes in the cake.

The gas carbon dioxide is a natural gas that occurs in air. It is plant food. We humans breathe in air with 0.04% carbon dioxide and breathe out air with 4% carbon dioxide. It is neither poisonous nor a pollutant. This is some of the real pollution in the modern world. Can you think of more?

Air pollution
Water pollution
Beach pollution
Ocean pollution
Plastic pollution
Chemical pollution
Littering
Light pollution
Noise pollution
Visual pollution
Electromagnetic pollution
Soil contamination
Radioactive contamination

> **KILLER KISS:**
>
> *If carbon dioxide was a poisonous pollutant, kissing someone could kill them because your breath contains 100 times more carbon dioxide than air. Put it to the test. Find someone you don't like and give them a big sloppy kiss. Don't try this with your dog unless you want to be licked.*

IQAir is a company that tracks global air quality for 131 countries. About 90% of all countries exceed the World Health Organisation air quality guidelines.

Only six countries and seven territories met the World Health Organisation guideline.

Poor countries had the worst air quality in 2021 and far exceeded the guidelines. The particles come from dust storms, de-vegetation, wildfires and poor hygiene and can produce lung and heart diseases.

Developing countries cannot afford to build well-engineered centralised coal-fired electricity generators with dust-capturing systems. Regulations and corruption are very different from those in wealthy countries.

Poverty and lack of cheap electricity has forced people to burn dung, twigs, leaves, wood and whatever they can find for hut heating and cooking. The air is filled with smoke composed of tiny particles. People, especially women and children like you, die from lung diseases and cancer.

The UN and EU wants to stop many poor countries, especially in Africa, from having cheap reliable coal-fired electricity. That's not fair.

You might not like doing homework but kids in Africa want a light to do homework. For them, a basic school education is the only way out of poverty and they can only dream of a university education.

> **DID YOU KNOW?**
> *A third of the people on the planet still use twigs, dung and wood for heating and cooking. You are one of the luckiest people on Earth.*

Do you want to swap places with a kid in a poor country? You too can cough yourself to death after a short life while you emit no carbon dioxide.

Or maybe you can do something to try to help people your age in those countries to have cheap, reliable coal-fired electricity. Banning the use of coal in these countries only kills more people. Is that fair?

Carbon dioxide is plant food yet we are told that carbon dioxide is a pollutant. As soon as the language has changed, you know you are not being told the truth.

Burning more fossil fuels per person means less polluted air, especially if you live in a wealthy democratic Western country.

This is a story you will never hear in the mainstream media. Why? Because it is good news and not some dreadful shock horror disaster.

SCHOOL STRIKES:
You held a banner "Climate action now". What does this really mean? Are you going to travel to China to demonstrate against the country that has the highest carbon dioxide emissions? Are you going to stop using your phone and computer? Will you stop eating? Will you walk everywhere? What will YOU do to make the world a better place?

Introduced plants and animals are one of the world's greatest pollutants. They kill and replace native plants and animals.

Most countries have thousands of invasive species. Some have been bought in deliberately for gardens and farming, some were introduced to solve another problem and others have arrived as stowaways on ships and in cargo.

Various types of fungus have been introduced to all countries from elsewhere. Rats and cats that have escaped from ships have killed off native bird and animal populations on isolated islands.

What a mess. There is almost no part of the world that does not have introduced plants and animals. Bushfires help to get rid of introduced plants and animals as

well as native plants and animals. Some native species regrow because they have adapted to fire.

If you really wanted to save the planet, you would go outside in the fresh air and pick up litter and kill introduced plants and animals. Why not go to the beach and collect plastic left lying around or washed up from the sea? These actions will make a difference.

Holding a banner at a school strike will make absolutely no difference, although it may be fun and is a good way of making new friends.

Each year there are emissions of carbon dioxide with 3% from human activities and 97% from natural emissions, mainly from the oceans, volcanoes and the breath of animals.

There are nearly 2,000 volcanoes above the ground, some of which leak out carbon dioxide. There are millions of known submarine volcanoes which emit huge amounts of carbon dioxide.

This carbon dioxide dissolves in cold, deep, high pressure, salty sea water and does not bubble to the surface. When currents bring deep seawater to the surface hundreds of years later, carbon dioxide goes from the water to the air.

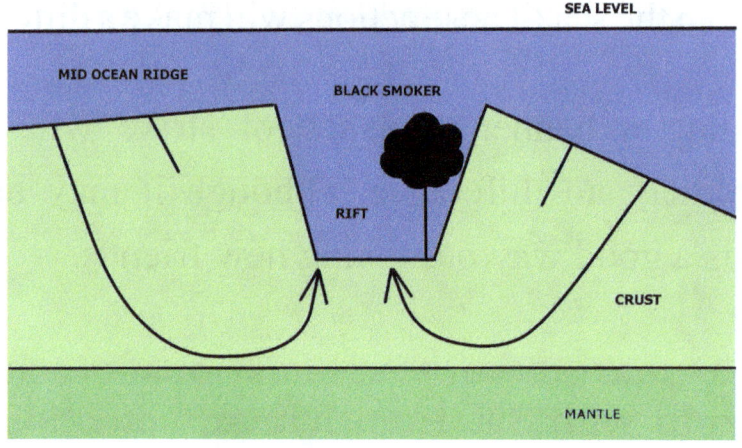

Carbon dioxide has been far higher in the past when icehouse conditions started. The past shows that carbon dioxide-rich air could not drive global warming, unless you want to change all the rules of chemistry and physics which operated in the past the same way as they do now. There is no relationship between carbon dioxide and temperature.

Sometimes we get told that we have had the hottest day for 10 years or since records began. The implication is that this is due to human activity. Wrong. The geological record shows us that the hottest days ever were 600, 500, 400, 200 and 100 million years ago. I think that these days were Thursdays.

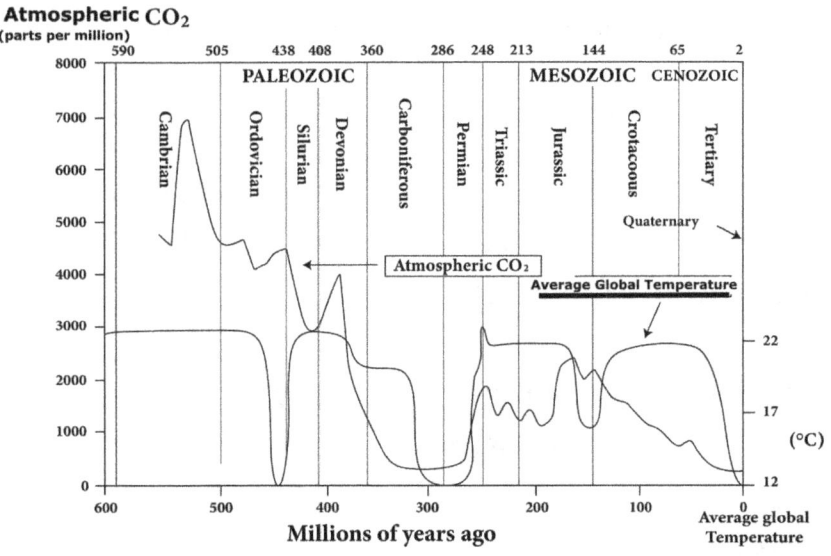

Diagram showing the decrease in carbon dioxide over the last 500 million years and the variation in temperature from hothouse to icehouse. We currently live in icehouse conditions.

Over the last 500 million years, temperature has been up and down many times between hothouse and icehouse conditions. The planet has been cooling for the last 50 million years and we are currently living in an icehouse.

Over the last 500 million years there has been a huge decrease in carbon dioxide in the air. If the trend continues and if carbon dioxide in air halves, all plants will die. Animals will have nothing to eat and will also die.

Carbon dioxide is innocent, don't lock it away.

Life thrived in past times when carbon dioxide in the air was high. The past shows that carbon dioxide does not drive temperature.

We have a very real problem with carbon dioxide in the air. There is just not enough of it and, unless you have a special kind of hatred for plants and animals, then you would not want to reduce or capture and bury carbon dioxide.

Carbon dioxide is a natural gas and could be in short supply for future plant life.

If we believe carbon dioxide drives global warming then, to save the planet and get out of the current icehouse, we should be putting as much carbon dioxide as possible back into the air by burning fossil fuels and cooking limestone to make cement.

Most coal deposits formed in periods during icehouse conditions when a giant supercontinent was over the South Pole.

Huge amounts of carbon dioxide were removed from air by plants in wetlands. Dead trees and leaves accumulated, were compacted to peat and then to coal.

Coal is fossilised sunlight that has locked away carbon dioxide that was in the air some 300 million years ago.

WHAT ROT:
Bacteria that decomposes wood today was not around when coal formed and so the dead wood, bark, twigs and leaves did not rot. This removed carbon dioxide from the air and stored it in the rock called coal. Burning coal puts carbon dioxide back to where it came from and feeds plants.

Coals rich in coalified wood are used for steam generation, coals rich in coalified waxy leaves are coking coals used for steel making and coals rich in pollen and spores are called oil shales. When heated, 1 tonne of oil shale produces up to 100 litres of oil.

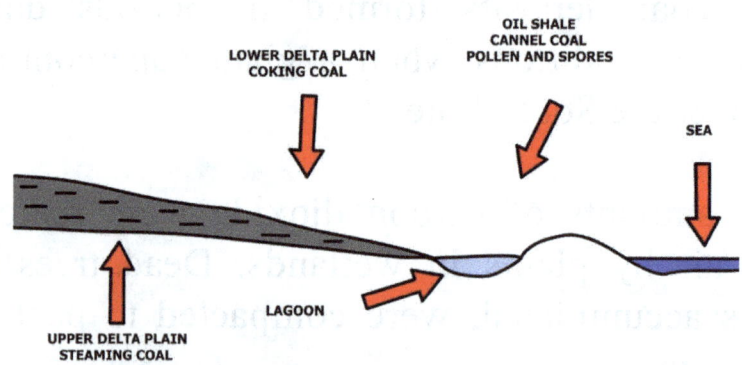

SAVE THE PLANET:

In Europe, the UK and USA, forests were chopped down to make charcoal for iron and glass making. As soon as coal was cheaper and became better for making steel and glass, the forests were no longer chopped down. They grew back. Most of the forests of Europe are regrowth forests. Coal saved the forests.

China is building six times as much coal-fired power as the rest of the world. Australia exports almost 400 million tonnes of coal each year for other countries to burn in power stations for electricity and to make steel.

At the same time, there is pressure in Australia to stop using Australian coal to make cheap reliable coal-fired electricity in Australia. Whatever Australia does, it makes no difference to the planet as Australia accounts for about 1% of annual human emissions of carbon dioxide.

Why bother doing anything unless big emitters like China and India stop using coal. Now.

EXTINCTION:

Australia has not built one coal-fired power station in 12 years and yet has bulldozed three and decommissioned another two coal-fired power stations. Australia is facing energy extinction.

The Western world cheers each time a coal-fired power station is closed. So does China because they then sell more and more polluting unreliable short-life wind turbines and solar panels to the Western world.

> **TROUBLEMAKING:**
> *Ask your school teacher if a steam engine is dinosaur technology. The wrong answer is "yes". Then ask how electricity is made using coal or uranium. They will probably tell you coal and nuclear power is bad.***

Most global carbon dioxide emissions come from the oceans as currents change and the oceans warm. At present, carbon dioxide in the air has been slightly increasing but has been decreasing over a very long time due to the formation of coal, limey shells, reefs, limey muds and carbon-rich muds.

**(HINT: Burning coal or the decay of uranium atoms generates heat which is used to make steam in a boiler. This is 200-year old technology. High pressure steam from the boiler spins a turbine which drives a spinning magnet in a coil to make an electric current. The chemical energy of coal is converted to heat energy which is then converted to electrical energy. Just because technology is old does not make it useless. The wheel is at least 5,500 years old and there would be no modern world without wheels.)

The bodies of dead tiny floating animals are trapped in muds and reefs. When more and more sediment is deposited in the oceans, these animals decompose to oil and gas.

This oil and gas may move from where it formed to be trapped in tiny holes in another rock or may stay trapped in mudstone or limestone.

To remove trapped oil and gas, the mudstone or limestone is broken by fracking, a process that has been used to produce oil and gas for 50 years.

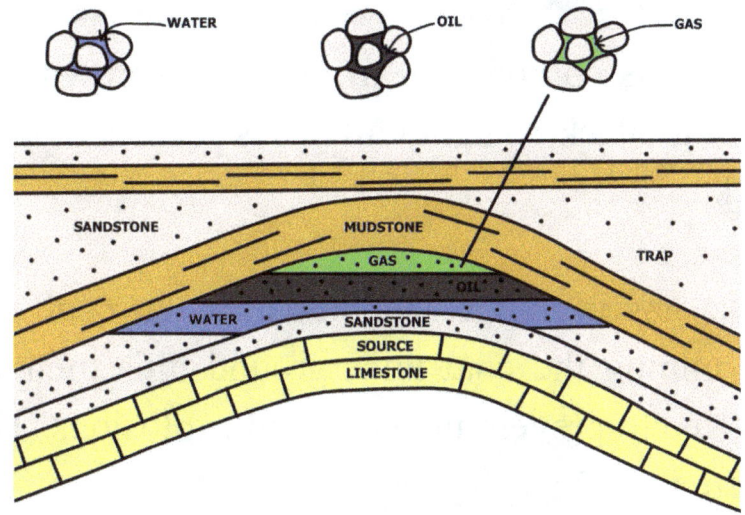

Water and household chemicals are forced at very high pressure into rocks at great depth. This makes cracks in the rock open up, quartz grains keep fractures open and trapped gas and oil is released. Minor earth tremors have been measured. Water is recovered and reused.

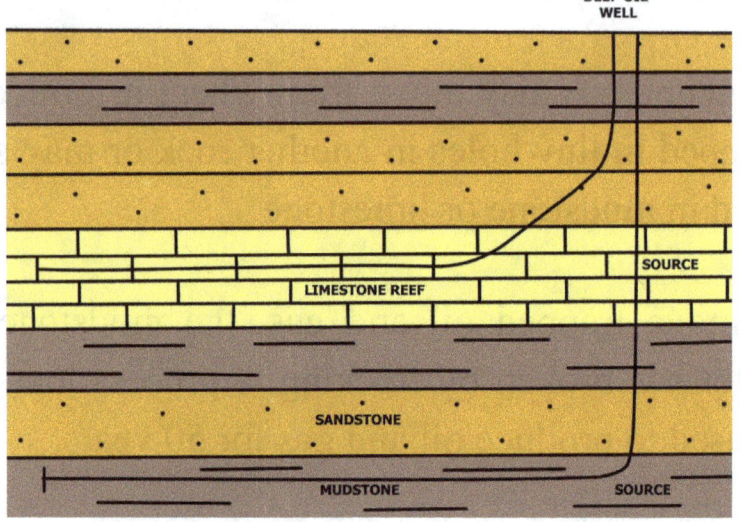

When coal is compressed from peat to brown coal and then to black coal, not all gas is squeezed out of the rock.

Methane gas is trapped in the cracks in coal and, before mining the coal underground, this methane is removed to prevent underground explosions. This has been done for 100 years.

After mining, bacteria and water can chemically

convert coal to methane gas which fills old coal mines. Never enter and old underground coal mine as there are both explosive and poisonous gases.

Drill holes into deep unmined coal remove methane coal seam gas for use in heating, cooking and making fertilisers, plastics and household chemicals.

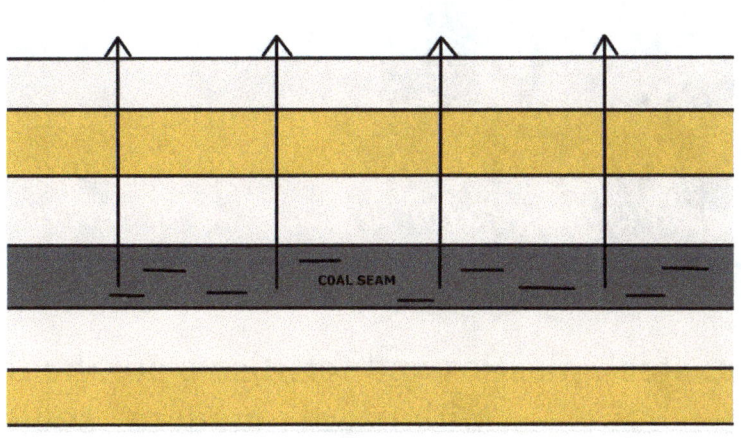

Carbon dioxide is plant food. Plants use carbon dioxide, sunlight, nutrients and water for photosynthesis. The more carbon dioxide in the air, the more plants grow, the less water they need and the less heat stress they endure.

In 2019, 4.5 billion tonnes of carbon dioxide was

released to the air to make cement. Steel making released 1.8 billion tonnes, plastics 370 million tonnes and ammonia for fertilisers 150 million tonnes.

Making these materials emitted 25% of human emissions and used 17% of the energy supply.

> **TREES:**
> *In Canada there are 318 billion trees that use 7.6 billion tonnes of carbon dioxide as food each year. Canadians release 545 million tonnes of carbon dioxide each year. Canada is already at Net Zero. Canadians pay tax for the amount of carbon dioxide they release.*

Cement, steel, plastics and fertilisers are the four pillars of modern society. Look around and see what you use made from cement, steel, plastics and fertilisers.

LIMESTONE + HEAT →
CARBON DIOXIDE + LIME

Would you survive in this modern world without these four essentials? The only solution for you is to live in a cave as a hunter-gatherer. How long would you last?

"Dad, why are we cold and sitting in the dark?"

"Because we have the miracle of green energy".

All plants use carbon dioxide as plant food. It's free. We humans eat plants and farm animals convert grass to meat and milk. Farmers, our food producers, are having more and more restrictions put on them by those who produce nothing.

TREES:
In USA, there are 228 billion trees that each year suck up 5.47 billion tonnes of carbon dioxide as plant food. Americans release 5 billion tonnes of carbon dioxide each year, 14% of the human global emissions. The US is already at Net Zero.

REALITY CHECK:
The best thing an apartment dweller can do is to take a holiday on a farm.

Air contains 0.04% carbon dioxide. Farmers burn propane gas and pump the warm exhaust fumes of carbon dioxide and water vapour into glasshouses. This increases the carbon dioxide in glasshouse air to 0.12%, the plants grow bigger, stronger and quicker and less water is used.

TREES:
In Australia, the grasslands, rangelands, forests, crops and continental shelf waters each year suck up ten times as much carbon dioxide than is released by Australians. Australia is already at Net Zero.

There have been thousands of experiments to show that plants grow much better when there is more carbon dioxide in the air.

The more plant food in the air the better. Farms become more efficient and less land needs to be cleared for farming.

> **TREES:**
> On planet Earth, there are 3 trillion trees that suck up 72 billion tonnes of carbon dioxide as plant food each year. Humans emit 37 billion tonnes of carbon dioxide each year. The planet is already at Net Zero, despite massive emissions from China. Floating algae in the oceans, crops and grass use even more carbon dioxide as plant food than trees.

By putting carbon dioxide in the air, we not only save the forests from being cut down for farm land but we help forests grow.

Growing food is energy intensive. Every process of food production uses energy whether it's diesel in a tractor for ploughing, seeding, weeding and harvesting; the electricity in the packing, milking or shearing shed; the energy used in mining, making and distributing fertiliser; transporting goods to the market; exporting food by ship or plane; keeping food cool in supermarkets 24/7; and transporting food home from where it was purchased.

Energy restrictions and Net Zero by governments make every process more expensive and food prices rise. Is that fair on people who have less than you?

> **LUNGS OF THE PLANET:**
> **Plants use carbon dioxide as food and release oxygen. The Amazon rainforests are often called the "lungs of the planet". They are not. Bacteria in the Amazon use almost half the oxygen produced by the trees to rot wood, twigs and leaves into humus. The lungs of the planet are floating green slime in the oceans. It's a bit hard to be a slime hugger. Don't believe me, try hugging slime and tell it that you love it.**

FRIEND OR FOE?
Is carbon dioxide your friend or foe? Silly question because you eat food.

Methane is a strong greenhouse gas. Most of the world's methane is released by rotting plants, especially in the Arctic. Huge amounts of methane are emitted from termites, soils and rocks. Some methane comes from leaks in gas pipelines and old coal mines and cattle burp out a small amount of methane.

Cattle eat grass. The carbon from the grass goes into meat, skin, bones, dung, urine, farts and burps. The carbon is recycled, most ends up back in the atmosphere and the process of cattle eating grass actually removes carbon from the air. There is also some recent scientific work that suggests methane contributes to global cooling. Make up your mind.

This does not stop activists and governments taxing cattle farmers even more for cattle burping out methane. The European Union wants to assassinate 200,000 cattle in Ireland because they burp out methane and don't even say excuse me.

Is this fair on Irish farmers? And what about you? You fart 15 times a day and each fart contains 7% methane. Simple solution: drop dead or glue up your bum.

YUK:
We are told cattle burps of methane are destroying the planet and, instead of eating beef, we should get our animal protein from insects. Try it. Then show me that eating insects can change the weather and climate. Don't forget to pick the bits of insect shell out of your teeth.

If there are rights for animals, then there should also be rights for insects.

Methane is a natural gas. Some of it leaks out from deep in the Earth. Methane is common on Titan, a moon of the outer planet Saturn. On Titan, not only does the atmosphere have methane but Titan has river channels and lakes of liquid methane.

QUESTION?
How do we know that there is methane on Titan if astronauts have never been there?

When methane burns, it produces heat, water vapour and carbon dioxide. Methane in the air quickly breaks down to water vapour and carbon dioxide. Methane is a strong greenhouse gas.

Why do we worry about minute traces of gas in air? There is 0.04% carbon dioxide, 0.00017% methane and 0.00003% nitrous oxide (laughing gas) in air. The bulk of these gases in air are from natural sources and humans only emit very small amounts. The main greenhouse gas in air is water vapour. Your breath contains 4% water vapour, air normally contains 2-3% water vapour and can be up to 4%.

DID YOU KNOW?
The greenhouse gas in the air that has the greatest effect is water vapour. Why have governments tried to ban methane and carbon dioxide emissions as greenhouse gases but not water vapour?

Activists started a war on laughing gas in Sri Lanka. Nitrogen fertilisers such as manufactured urea or ammonium nitrate were banned by the government and insisted that "natural" fertilisers like dung be used.

It only took one growing season for crop failure, starvation, riots and a forced change of the Sri Lankan government.

The Netherlands tried to close farms because of emissions of laughing gas from crops. This led to political changes and demonstrations.

It is only in the last 100 years we learnt how to stop starvation. It is still lurking just around the corner. If there was global cooling, an energy crisis, no fertilisers, a supervolcano, a Carrington event or an asteroid impact, then many plants and animals, including humans, would starve. It's too terrible to think about it. Just laugh, love and live.

OUCH: Next time you go to the dentist, refuse to have laughing gas as an anaesthetic in order to save the planet. You won't be laughing.

It has taken thousands of years of experiments to create fertilisers that make farming far more efficient and less labour intensive. This resulted in more food and less clearing of forests. Synthetic nitrogen fertilisers have saved the forests.

NITROGEN SUICIDE:
If we did not use synthetic nitrogen fertilisers, the land area for food production would have to double or the population would have to halve. Why don't activists who want nitrogen fertilisers banned lead by example and just shuffle off.

GO AWAY: If you want Net Zero and stop using fossil fuels, then get out of my life and go and live in a cave as a hunter-gatherer.

The best modern example of Net Zero is North Korea. Compared to the adjacent South Korea, there is no electricity for lighting, cooking, heating, cooling and jobs. I'm not going to do everything for you, look up a satellite photo of the Korean Peninsula at night.

Germany tried to transition from fossil fuels to renewables on the path to Net Zero. Days with wind calm, snow and dust on solar panels and the shutting down of reliable cheap coal, gas and nuclear power stations pushed energy costs through the roof. People died.

Many collected firewood from forests for heating and cooking. Germans, who love their cars, were forced to drive electric cars they didn't want to drive rather than internal combustion engine cars which have monumentally improved in efficiency over the last century.

Germany in 2023 was in a recession, food

prices went through the roof, jobs were lost and industries moved to other countries.

Germany now relies on Russian gas, French nuclear energy, Polish coal-fired electricity and Norwegian hydropower. Because they now don't control their own future, Germany decided to restart their closed coal-fired and nuclear power stations.

The average person has become poor and a few elite people have become even richer and more powerful. This was a predictable own goal for the Germans.

OIL SAVED THE PLANET:
In the early 1900s, city roads were covered in horse poo which washed into water wells. People died of bacterial, viral and parasite infections. Once fossil fuel-driven cars replaced horses, the amount of horse poo in cities decreased. Fossil fuel cars saved people dying of disease in cities.

Only 45% of fossil fuels are used for gasoline (petrol). In our day-to-day life we use more than 6,000 chemicals made from fossil fuels in things such as toothpaste, cosmetics, paints, mobile phones, computers and asphalt on roads.

SAVE THE PLANET:
Whales were hunted almost to extinction to be cut up and boiled to make whale oil for lanterns. Some traditional cultures still hunt whales for food. Fossil fuel oil replaced whale oil in lamps and whales were saved from extinction. It was fossil fuels that saved the whales, not greens

INTERNET SEARCH:
Look up what we use in everyday life made from fossil fuels. Now tell me what you are going to give up in order to save the planet.

To make a bottle of water, one litre of oil and seven litres of water are used. To make one litre of bottled water, 600 times as much carbon dioxide is emitted compared to making one litre of tap water. If you want to save the planet, drink tap water.

HUG A PLUMBER:
Tap water and sewage systems have saved more lives than medicine.

Drink bottles account for 38% of rubbish volume in landfill. In Western countries, a litre of bottled water costs thousands of times more than tap water.

In previous centuries, people died from the simple act of drinking water. Once dams, pumping stations and pipes were built and bacteria in water were killed, people did not die from drinking water.

In Third World countries today, people still die

from cholera, diarrhoea, dysentery, hepatitis A, typhoid and polio just from drinking water.

SAVE THE PLANET:
Recycling just one plastic water bottle saves enough energy to power a television for 90 minutes.

Is there really an energy transition from fossil fuels to renewables occurring? For the last 100 years, more than 80% of all energy used by humans has come from fossil fuels. They do the heavy lifting, wind and solar can't compete.

The Western countries burn more fossil fuels per person than poor countries. Western countries have the cleanest air on the planet.

Singapore emits 89,420 tonnes of carbon dioxide per square kilometre, the highest in the world. Singapore has changed from a filthy dirty diseased country to one of the cleanest countries in the world in just 60 years. This was done by becoming wealthy.

> **SAVE THE PLANET:**
> Human and animal muscles were used for the hard work in farming. Children like you worked hard all-day every-day in the fields, forests and mines. Once coal-fired steam engines were invented, the amount of muscle work by humans and animals decreased. More efficient diesel farm machines replaced coal-fired machines. New technology and fossil fuels have saved humans and animals from being worked to death.

Net Zero is a First World aim of having no carbon dioxide emissions. It is an impossible impractical dream of wealthy people who want to feel good. No poor people in Third World countries want Net Zero. They are already at Net Zero.

Net Zero for Western countries will make everyone poorer and a few people even richer. Is this what you really want in your life? Is this fair?

DID YOU KNOW?:
Technology advances benefit women more than men. The change from human energy to mechanised energy has meant that traditional tasks of women such as hand grinding grain to flour, gathering food, collecting firewood, washing clothing by hand, cooking over a fire and gathering water now don't exist. Women have more freedoms and time now. Net Zero will bring us back to these old ways. Is this fair?

By keeping people constantly fearful and anxious about a mythical climate catastrophe, people can be controlled.

With Net Zero, you would have no hot showers, you would have to walk to a polluted river to collect water, your toilet would be the bush, there would be no hot meals, no storage of food in a refrigerator, no meat, no holidays, no television or internet, no mobile phone, no computers, no electric lights, no home heating or cooling and no clothes except those made from animal skins or grass.

You would walk everywhere and you would hunt and gather your food from the forest. How long would you last?

> **DID YOU KNOW?:**
> Three billion people use less electricity each day than a refrigerator. We need more cheap reliable electricity to save the planet.

Don't try to say Kandahalagalaa while sneezing.

Drill holes into this uninhabited coral atoll in the Maldives in the Indian Ocean show that sea level was a few metres higher than now only 5,000 years ago. After that, sea level went up and down by 0.9 metres well before humans started to emit carbon dioxide.

Start eating a cookie and try to say the names of the other coral atolls that show the same: Mainadhoo, Baavanadhoo, Kondey, Vaadhoo, Dhakandhoo, Hulhudhoo, Thiladhoo, Cocos-Keeling, Warrebar, Berwick, Lady Elliot, Mba, Tepuka, Tutaga, Laura, Jabat, Jeh, Jabnodren, Jin, Malamaia, Navini and Makin.

Most of the 1,100 Indian and Pacific Ocean atolls are growing. Some tiny islands are shrinking and big islands are growing or stable. Now, tell me again about the scary stories about island and atoll nations being inundated by rising sea levels.

Geologist Charles Lyell showed in 1833 that atolls grow as sea level rises. Charles Darwin's 1842 book on atolls showed the same.

Edgeworth David's drilling of the Funafuti atoll in 1896-1898 confirmed Lyell's theory as did drilling of the Bikini Atoll between 1954-1958.

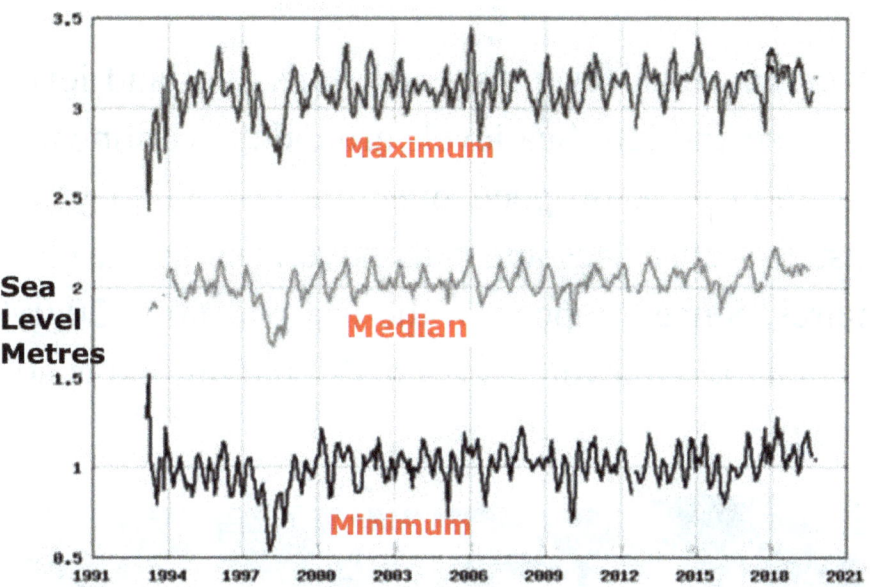

Sea level measurements at the Funafuti Atoll, Tuvalu. Maybe Pacific atoll nations saw a new way of making money by demanding that Western countries pay compensation for potential future sea level rise and inundation.

Satellite measurements over the last 40 years show atolls are expanding and sea level measurements show that there is no inundation.

The scare story of atoll inundation is deliberate disinformation but it does not stop the story getting wide media coverage. Have you ever seen a correction of this story in the media?

Over time, sea level rises and falls and land levels also rise and fall. Sea levels around the continent of Australia have dropped over the last 5,000 years. Past sea level rises and falls have been at least 600 metres. Since the peak of the last glaciation 20,000 years ago, sea level has risen 130 metres and is still rising.

QUESTION:
The iron age city of Lydia is now under the Aegean Sea in Turkey. Has global sea level risen or the land sunk over the last 3,000 years?

QUESTION:
The Roman port of Efeses in Turkey is 4 metres above sea level. Has global sea level fallen or has the land risen over the last 2,000 years?

In Sydney Harbour, Fort Denison was built on the rocky island of Pinchgut during the Crimean War (1853-1856). It was to stop the Russian navy entering Sydney Harbour. Building was completed after the Crimean War finished.

A tidal measuring station shows there that over the last 160 years, there has only been a millimetre or two change in sea level. Fort Denison has done a fantastic job. It kept out the Russian navy and stopped sea level rise.

If someone is telling you about sea level rise without, in the same breath, telling you about land level rises and falls, then they are not speaking the truth.

GREAT BARRIER REEF:
There is more coral in the Great Barrier Reef of Australia now than in previous times. This is because there have been fewer cyclones than previously.

The Great Barrier Reef of Australia has had the highest coral cover since measurements began 36 years ago yet we are told it is endangered and facing extinction. We have had reefs on Earth for 3,500 million years. They come, they go, and are generally killed off by sea level fall, cold climates or volcanic ash.

The Great Barrier Reef has appeared and disappeared many times before humans were on Earth. The main back-reef sediment is reef material broken up by cyclones and not sediment from farmlands inland. In Great Barrier Reef waters, no pesticides or farm chemicals have been detected despite scary stories by activists.

No country runs on sea breezes and sunbeams for their electricity. It is not possible because wind and solar do not deliver the grunt to run a modern society.

Because the community had been panicked about how burning coal to make electricity produces carbon dioxide which will lead to unstoppable global warming, massive new business opportunities arose.

New energy players appeared, built wind turbines and solar panels here, there and everywhere and justified what they did because they were saving the planet.

Turbines and solar panels are big business and destroy the environment and don't change climate. Worldwide, they receive more than $600 million a day in subsidies. Governments fell for the hype and used taxpayer's money to subsidise what was called renewable energy.

Western countries were speared with wind turbines and good farming land was covered with solar panels. We were told that the wind and the Sun are free and renewable energy was the cheapest form of energy available.

This is not true because wind and solar generators last a short time and have to be replaced after less than 20 years. Coal and nuclear electricity generators last at least 60 years. **The more renewable energy was added to the grid, the more electricity prices rose.**

It does not matter how many wind turbines or solar panels there are, if the wind does not blow at night then fossil fuel or nuclear energy are needed to keep systems going all night. Batteries only last minutes to an hour or so.

Are solar and wind energy renewable or ruinable? Are they good for the environment? No. Do they lower emissions of carbon dioxide? **No.**

The only thing renewable about renewable energy are the subsidies. They just keep coming and coming and are hidden in a highly complex electricity pricing structure and taxes.

The subsidies come from employers, taxpayers and electricity users. The wealthier a country becomes, the more electricity is used per person and the less polluted the country.

> **HOW TO REDUCE ELECTRICITY USE:**
>
> *Turn off heating, air conditioning, refrigerators, computers, lights, smart phone chargers and walk everywhere. Easy. Try it for the rest of the year.*

The energy used to make a wind or solar facility is

far greater than the energy they will ever produce. Why bother?

The carbon dioxide emissions from manufacturing wind and solar facilities are far more than emissions saved by closing coal-fired power stations.

> *It's a proven scientific fact that toast triangles taste far better than toast squares. Prove me wrong.*

Wind turbine blades slice and dice bats and birds and create health problems for those living nearby. Offshore wind turbines are far bigger, kill whales and drop oil into the oceans.

Wind turbines destroy scenic views and are a navigation hazard. Pristine rainforest inland from the Great Barrier Reef has been flattened to build a wind complex. Is this environmentalism?

The wind does not constantly blow. There are long periods of time when there is no wind, called wind droughts. This has been known by sailors for thousands of years.

> **DID YOU KNOW:**
> *There were days during the wind drought in 2021 in Europe and the UK that there was no wind power. Electricity prices went through the roof and people had to rely on nuclear-, coal- and gas-generated electricity. Before the introduction of renewable energy, this did not happen.*

Turbine blades are layers of wood and epoxy resin. To make blades, Amazon rainforest balsa trees need to be cut down and highly toxic chemicals in epoxy resins such as **bisphenol-A** are used in the blades.

Bisphenol-A is banned in many countries, the blades erode and spread bisphenol-A far and wide into soils and the waterways and the blades cannot be recycled after their short life. Blades are cut up, dumped and bisphenol-A leaks into soils and waterways.

Is this what you want? Emissions of the plant food carbon dioxide are far better for the planet.

The rare earth elements used in wind turbines are mined in China, the radioactive uranium- and thorium-rich wastes are dumped and spread over a wide area of land. Most turbine blades are manufactured in communist China.

If you are a supporter of wind power for environmental reasons, you are also responsible for radioactive contamination of large areas of the planet.

DID YOU KNOW?
In 2018 wind added no electricity to the UK grid for nine days. Power prices went through the roof. No country runs on wind.

It is not possible to be an environmentalist and support the generation of electricity from wind turbines, unless of course you are a hypocrite or are making money in the wind business. Wind turbines are catastrophic for the environment.

It will be your generation that is responsible for cleaning up the mess made by your parent's generation in the name of environmentalism. This is a case of having to destroy the environment to save the plant.

DID YOU KNOW?
Scottish wind turbines are warmed by burning fossil fuels to stop them freezing in cold weather. Hydraulic oil is spread everywhere. Are wind turbines saving the planet from fossil fuels?

Slave labour in China makes silicon solar panels. Poisonous heavy metals in solar panels are spread over huge areas every time it rains. Prime agricultural land for production of food is covered with thousands of hectares of solar panels. This is not environmentalism.

BARGAIN BASEMENT CORNER:
Hurry hurry hurry, queue here to buy solar panels made by slave labour that are guaranteed to make the weather cooler in 80 years time. Or is it 100 years? Or maybe 200 years? Don't ask questions, just give me your money.

When the Sun's rays hit solar panels, electricity and heat are generated. In many places during summer, the panels overheat and can't be used.

Electricity from coal-fired generators needs to be used for air conditioning, fans, refrigerators, cooking and just to keep the lights on when the Sun does not shine for a while, at night or when solar panels are turned off.

Those supporting solar electricity claim that solar energy will reduce global warming. If the panels must be shut down when it's warm, then they are useless in preventing global warming.

Demand your government make the Sun shine at night so that solar power can be efficient.

More than $10 trillion has been spent over the last two decades trying to make wind and solar work. They still provide only 2.1% of global energy. For this amount of money, all of Europe could have been rebuilt after being flattened in World War 2.

Solar and wind energy do not provide the 24/7 electricity generated from coal, nuclear, gas or hydro. There needs to be back up for solar and wind.

Battery back-up is prohibitively expensive and only provides power, at most, for an hour or so. No city has ever operated on batteries.

> **DID YOU KNOW?**
> *A ham and cheese sandwich priced at $4 is around 30 times more energy-dense weight-for-weight than the best lithium battery priced at $500.*

To build a 100 MW gas turbine, 300 tonnes of iron ore, 2,000 tonnes of concrete and 100 tonnes of special metals are used on an area the size of a household block.

To build a 100 MW wind turbine complex, 30,000 tonnes of iron ore, 30,000 tonnes of concrete, 1,000 tonnes of special metals and 800 tonnes of plastics are used in an area of 26 square kilometres of land.

Which technology is better for the environment?

The land footprint of solar and wind energy systems is enormous compared to coal, gas and nuclear generation footprints. Environmentalism should be about making the smallest footprint on the planet. Why cover food producing land with solar panels?

DID YOU KNOW?
Wind turbines weigh 100 to 300 tonnes and can be up to 700 tonnes. Turbines in coal-fired generators weigh 600 tonnes. Wind turbines last no more than 20 years, turbines in coal-fired and nuclear generators last at least 60 years. Wind turbines require massive maintenance compared to coal- and nuclear-fired turbines. Why do you think wind power is far more expensive that coal and nuclear electricity? Is it because the wind does not blow all the time? Is it because turbines require far more maintenance? Is it because the life of a wind turbine is very short?

If you believe that human emissions drive global warming, for which there is no evidence, then you must be a passionate supporter of nuclear power.

Wind, solar and hydro damage the environment and, of course, coal and gas cannot be used because burning these fossil fuels allegedly creates emissions. Why aren't green activists pushing for nuclear power?

The power density of fossil fuel and nuclear generators is about the same order of magnitude as the total power for the average tornado. Wind and solar power density are about the same as a horse.

Wind and solar facilities are built in remote areas. Why not in cities, along beaches and harbours and in parks close to the users? Is it because city people think that they are ugly and destroy the environment?

If so, don't build them. Anywhere. A new grid needs to be built to carry electricity from remote areas to the users in cities. Why build a second grid when there is already a grid?

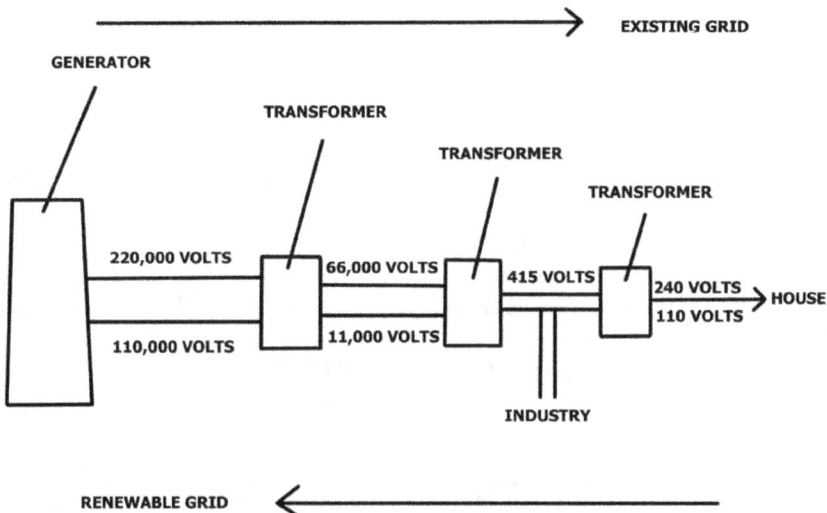

Voltage losses are reduced when electricity is transmitted using high voltage. Wind and solar generation are in remote areas at the low voltage end of the grid and, if a country is to be run on wind and solar, the grid needs to be rebuilt and reversed.

Why ask Third World countries to give up the cheapest form of energy and remain in dire poverty with malnutrition, preventable disease and high premature deaths? Global warming policy is not fair and kills people.

We are in an energy crisis. There is abundant energy but it is being mismanaged with activists, politicians and bureaucrats running energy systems rather than electrical engineers.

Energy bills have risen before because of substitution of cheap reliable coal and nuclear power by wind and solar. As a result, there may be a food, financial or social crisis.

Climate cycles show that past climate changes are due to the position of the continents, the Earth's address in the galaxy, the orbit of the Earth and the variable amount of energy released by the Sun.

The past shows us that we have reached the peak of an interglacial in the current long ice age and are in a long-term cooling cycle.

All the scary doom and gloom predictions about future warming are based on models predicting future climate and not measurements.

Many assumptions are made in making a model. Big problems trying to model climate are that clouds get in the way, models assume carbon dioxide is the driver of climate and the past is not considered.

More than 100 climate models have been floating around for the last 40 years. We've been able to compare the model with measurements of what actually happened. The models failed.

The models were unable to predict future temperature, no matter what sized supercomputer was used.

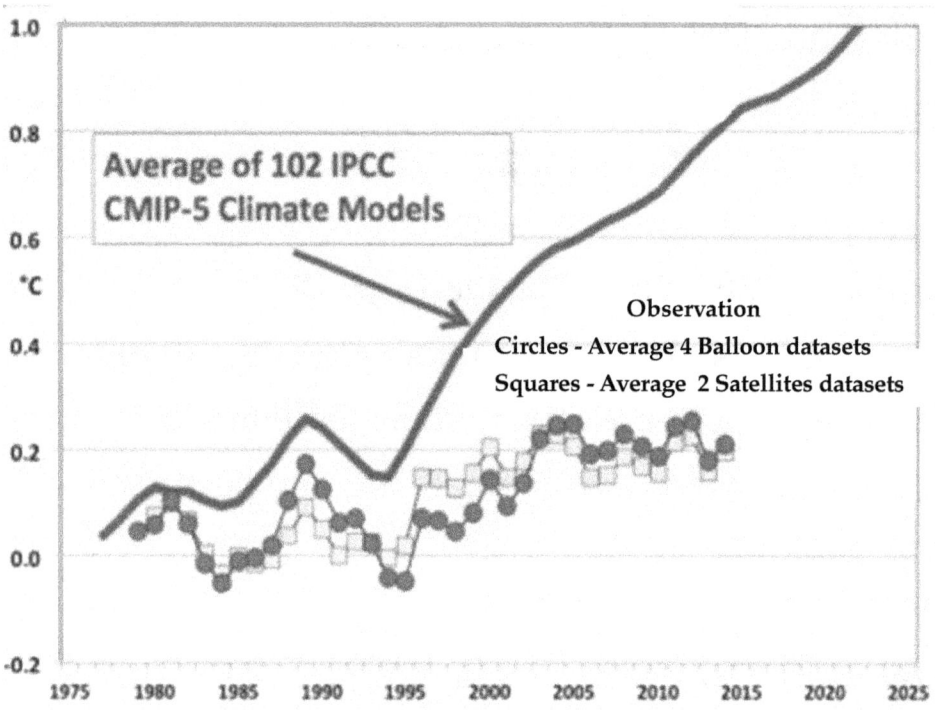

Diagram of the last 40 years of the average of 102 IPCC climate model predictions and the actual temperature change over this time measured from satellites and balloons.

Political decisions about energy source, distribution and costs are based on models that don't work. To make matters worse, no one has even shown that human emissions of carbon dioxide drive global warming. You've been conned in a sea of disinformation.

Billions have been spent on wind and solar generating systems yet electricity prices have risen massively. Why should economic growth be slowed on a possible eventuality based in models which don't work?

Global warming policy is a threat to prosperity and social cohesion with huge strains placed on the state and people by a flawed consensus on global warming.

The cost of this sugar hit will not hurt me as I am in the last 20% of my life but it will hurt you because you are in the first 20% of your life.

Your future relies on climate models that don't work. They create high electricity prices, the cost of everything rises, the number of good jobs decreases and climate policy will prevent you from buying your own house. You can't live at home forever, you need to get a life.

Climate change policy is one of the most costly and undemocratic policy mistakes for generations. A previous one was communism.

Climate change activism is the greatest scientific mistake made for generations. A previous one was Lysenkoism in communist Soviet Union which led to the death by starvation of at least 30 million people. People were imprisoned and killed for disagreeing with Lysenko's rejection of genetics. All scientists agree when you censor, imprison or kill those who don't.

We often hear the view that 97% of scientists believe that global warming is of human origin. Why not check the original source? A survey of 10,000 climate "scientists" received 3,000 replies of which 77 were chosen and 76 said that human emissions change the climate.

> **JOKE OR SERIOUS?**
> *All scientists agree when the ones that disagree are censored. Therefore, 97% of all climate scientists agree with the government that funds them.*

Brains are a commodity and can be bought and sold at will. Character, bravery, honesty and loyalty derive from breeding. You never have to remember anything if you speak the truth.

I am regarded as controversial because I use facts and speak the truth. Those who disagree abuse me rather than using facts to support their arguments. I would rather be abused for speaking the truth and using facts than to have to live with a lie.

An increase in carbon dioxide in the air has led to the greening of the Sahara and better crop yields. If climate change is beneficial or only slight in its effects, then the climate activist scientists would not have received billions of dollars of taxpayer's money. These so-called climate "scientists" would be out of work unless they frightened taxpayers into paying them more money.

If you cannot model natural climate change, you have no idea what the human influence on climate is. Why waste trillions of dollars to stop a hypothetical climate change? Your generation will be in poverty until they pay back the debt from this stupidity.

Soon you will be able to frighten politicians with your vote. A frightened politician is a good politician. They are more interested in the perks of the job, re-election and looking after their mates. Put their feet to the fire and make them sweat. Don't have your future killed off by politicians who won't be around when you suffer.

There is no reason or urgent need to reduce our carbon dioxide emissions. For the last 120 years, fossil fuels have given us more than 80% of the energy we use. They still do.

If a future energy source such as nuclear fusion is used, we will continue to use fossil fuels for the 6,000 materials made from fossil fuels we use in everyday life.

Maybe you should ask teachers, environmental activists and politicians who are telling you about a climate crisis to show you how they live.

Do they eat farmed food? Do they drive anywhere? Do they fly anywhere? Do they have house heating and cooling? Do they have a phone, computer or television? Do they live in a cave? It's a case of do as I say but not do as I do.

You soon will be ready for your first car. You do not reduce emissions or save the planet by driving an electric vehicle (EV). It's the exact opposite. Driving an EV solves nothing, creates unforeseen problems, costs a bomb and is highly inefficient. Don't buy a second-hand EV unless you own a gold mine.

It takes 80,000 km of driving to pay back the amount of carbon dioxide emitted to make an EV.

EVs use six times as much metal as conventional cars. Going green by using an EV requires far more and far larger mines than exist at present. That metal has to be mined and transported using diesel-driven machines. The electricity used to change EVs comes from coal-fired generators.

If the world's 1.5 billion vehicles are swapped with EVs, we would need 944 million tonnes of lithium. We only have 26 million tonnes of lithium reserves on the planet. What happens if someone somewhere invents a better battery using say vanadium?

> **LITHIUM:**
> *Not enough lithium has been found in the world, the price of lithium has risen 800 times and the lithium required for future EVs has yet to be found, mined and processed.*

A huge amount of copper is used in EVs. We have not yet discovered the copper deposits needed to produce the copper for EVs. Most will be found in Third World countries. The great rich copper deposits have already been found at the surface. They are now being mined or have been mined out.

We are now mining rocks with less and less copper and at greater depths. This produces even larger waste dumps and tailings dams with minerals that react with water and air to produce acid drainage.

By driving an EV you must be a huge supporter of the mining industry and are responsible for the environmental mess in poor Third World countries. Feel good?

Lithium batteries in EVs use cobalt mined by black slave children in the Congo. Many die in dangerous deep open cuts and underground mines. Others are poisoned by cobalt. China controls the cobalt mining in the Congo.

When you swan around in your EV feeling morally superior to those in their fossil fuel vehicles, do you ever spare a thought for the child slaves that died to provide metal for your EV? They were your age. Is that fair?

EVs were tried in the 1830s and failed. They were tried in the early 1900s and failed. Then, as now, they were too heavy, too hard to recharge and could not go very far.

China controls the basic commodities used in EVs such as lithium, cobalt, nickel and graphite. It is now the biggest car manufacturer in the world.

> *EVs:*
> **Governments 30 years ago tried to force people to buy diesel cars to save the planet. Now the same governments are saying that diesel cars are bad for the environment and we must buy EVs.**

In the UK, drivers are buying petrol and diesel vehicles. There is a lack of charging stations, massive loss of value after purchase of a very high cost vehicle, eye-wateringly high repair costs and difficulties in travel, even small distances and especially in winter.

Safety features such as being unable to get out of the car when it runs out of charge and battery fires make EVs unattractive. Governments are trying to force people to drive EVs without investing the trillions of dollars necessary to change the electricity grid. That's money that could go into building a house for you.

EV insurers are reluctant to attempt repairs for even the most minor battery damage which can be caused by something as small as mounting the kerb. EVs are written off because there are so few technicians qualified to safely repair EVs. Is this environmentalism?

Because of the fire risk, some ferry owners refuse to carry EVs and some car parks don't allow EVs.

EVs don't go far, the battery degrades quickly, a huge amount of time is wasted with charging, there are few charging stations, they cost a fortune, maintenance and insurance is crippling, they are worth next to nothing after a few years use, they catch alight and whole new electricity grids need to be built to charge EVs.

If you cared for the environment and your fellow humans, you would not use cobalt and would not drive an EV that was destined for landfill after a short life.

HOW TO SPOT PROPAGANDA DRESSED UP AS SCIENCE: Sensational headlines, conclusions not in accord with previous validated work, selective reporting and results that can't be replicated.

There is no such thing as a consensus or settled science. New discoveries keep being made. We once thought toluene and benzene over the vast areas of the Southern Ocean was pollution from the oil industry.

Recently it was discovered that blooms of phytoplankton release these chemicals into clouds. This information was not used in climate models that support a $1.5 trillion climate industry dependent upon the accuracy of models.

We've seen many previous examples of settled science such as: The Earth is flat; the Earth is the centre of the universe; the atom is the smallest particle in the universe; the electron is the smallest sub-atomic particle; global cooling and now global warming.

We've also seen many scary predictions. All were wrong. In the 1960s, we were told oil would be gone in 10 years. More oil continues to be found and it is still being used in increasing amounts.

In the 1970s, we were told we are facing an ice age in 10 years. It didn't happen. We were also told that there would be famine and depopulation of the planet. The exact opposite has happened.

In the 1980s, we were told that forests would be wiped out and crops would fail because of acid rain. Since then, the global forest area and food production have increased. In the 1990s, we were told we would fry and die because of the ozone hole. We didn't.

In the 2000s, we were told that there would be no snow and the ice caps would melt in 10 years. Another dud prediction. In the 2010s, we were told that we will fry and die and the dams would never fill with water. **Total BS.**

There is always someone trying to big note themselves with scary predictions. This has been happening for thousands of years. If just one end-of-the-world prediction was correct, you would not be here.

As soon as you hear a doomsday prediction, don't even bother to argue. The people making them were probably dropped on their head too many times as a child.

Governments like to keep people frightened. They can get credit for saving them from a non-problem and control people. Don't fall for it. They spend trillions of dollars of your money to fix something that's not broken using disinformation. This money could be better spent on schools, health, housing, hospitals and real environmentalism.

Arguments are won by discussion using logic and facts and not by vandalism or "look at me" exhibitionism. In most Western countries, there is the right to protest. This is not a right to disrupt or destroy.

There have been 27 Conference of the Parties (COP) meetings. Tens of thousands of people claiming to be vitally concerned about carbon dioxide emissions meet in exotic international resorts.

Hundreds travelled by carbon dioxide-emitting private jets and tens of thousands in carbon dioxide-emitting commercial jets, cars and ships to stay in luxury resorts that have air conditioning, heating and exotic foods and fluids flown in from all over the world.

The wealthy elite emit many times more carbon dioxide than us and yet they tell us to emit less plant food, become poorer and lose freedoms.

Since the start of these COP talk-fests, the global human emissions of carbon dioxide have risen. COP have achieved absolutely nothing but those who we paid to attend had great party times with all their friends at our expense.

Politicians and COP party attendees are planning to lower emissions by 2050. They won't be around then to be accountable for their actions. You will.

Force politicians tell us what climate changes will occur in 2025, 2026, 2027, 2028 and each year after that as a result of their climate actions today.

We live in the best times ever to be a human on planet Earth. There is more food; less disease; more money; we live longer and we have energy for growing, transporting, heating and cooling food; and we have energy for lights, transport and everything we use. We can have hot showers each day. We can travel in fossil fuel-burning vehicles, aeroplanes and ships.

The internet uses about 8% of the world's energy. Making fertiliser for food uses about 2% of the world's energy. What would you do without the internet, food, travel, hot water, house heating and cooling and your phone?

If you were really concerned about your climate footprint, then you must give up everything you do and use in your modern life.

We had Net Zero with humans being beasts of burden until machines did the hard work. If you didn't work, you didn't eat and if you didn't eat, you died.

There was no such thing as single mother pensions, unemployment benefits, sick leave, disability pensions or old age pensions. You were on your own to sink or swim.

Children did much of the hard work in the fields, in underground mines and in factories. Many children died doing hard work.

Slavery has not stopped. There are more slaves today than ever before in history. What have you done to stop slavery?

What rights don't you have? In most countries in the world, people don't have the rights you have. In Western countries only 250 years ago, there were no rights for women, gays, children and most men. People could not vote. Property ownership was only for the filthy rich. Later, in the 1850s, only 5% of men in the world could vote. Women then could not vote.

Your government has a duty to provide you with the cheapest and most reliable energy and not to look after their mates. It's your right but it's not happening.
.

How can you demonise carbon when all life and food contains carbon? Save the planet is code for give us your money and give us control of every aspect of your life. Just say no.

Anxiety, fear and depression are strong emotions today. Get rid of these emotions and replace them with laughter, love and living life.

A climate change crisis or climate emergency is a concocted First World scare story that is repeated over and over and over and over so that you might eventually believe the scare story. If the scare story has to be repeated so many times, then it is propaganda.

There is a crisis in common sense. Not a climate crisis.

for parents and grandparents

We are all environmentalists. We want a better planet for ourselves and future generations. We do not want to be manipulated, lied to or bombarded with exaggerated hysteria about the state of the planet. In my life of more than three score and ten years, the planet in my neck of the woods has got better because of greater wealth, technology and environmental awareness.

I have seen a huge improvement in air, water and soil quality; a change from reusing everything because of poverty to recycling; better, more efficient and cheaper consumables and cars; better, more diverse and cheaper food; better health and greater longevity; more disposable cash and the ability to travel cheaply with ease to places we could only dream about when young. The streets are no longer used as effluent drains and places to dump rubbish.

In my lifetime, I have seen the appearance of plumbing systems for water and sewage, extensive public transport, sealed roads and cheap reliable employment-generating electricity. As we became wealthier and wealthier, we used more and more energy and polluted less. As children, we couldn't wait to be an adult in the new modern world and there was no such thing as ecoanxiety.

This book is for parents and grandparents to read and show to children. Scientific references to all facts in this book are in *Heaven and Earth* and are basic undergraduate geology. It is hard for children to escape from the clutches of incessant negative emotionally-disturbing propaganda that they receive at school regarding the health of the planet. This brain washing propaganda and disinformation exploits vulnerability and is easily recognised by jargon, disorganised phrases, negativity, constant repetition and a lack of logic. It is an attempt to change the world into a place with serfs controlled by unelected elites.

It's time to deprogram children and hit the reset button. Schools have now become the playgrounds for activists and weirdos promoting an unhealthy view of the family, gender, sex and science. The weirdos are coming for your children. Children should be learning about the long history of our planet. Kids are learning from playing computer games created by evil people. With some, the solution to a problem is violence and killing and they become desensitised. This is another classroom for children.

School should be fun with young people given the basics for survival in later life and places where young people are taught to question, think critically and analytically and commit a large body of knowledge to memory. The social, ethical, political and religious ideas should be moulded at home in a family setting. However, this is becoming increasingly difficult because, in many western countries, the extended family structure has broken down and children become ripe for the picking by cult-like figures.

Education is for life and should produce self-sufficient citizens.

We spend our lives dealing with snake oil salesmen trying to con us and children need to be able to argue, see the fallacy of bland statements and meaningless chants and know how to ask incisive questions such as "Show me the evidence?" Children need to be trained to spot snake oil at 100 paces.

If a child "Googles it" or uses Wikipedia, then they can be exposed to a body of corrupted biased selective information that is often demonstrably wrong. They are certainly not gaining knowledge. This book provides a few uncomfortable and obscure facts, asks questions that children should be asking and exposes children to the thread that underpins all science: scepticism.

As a parent and grandparent, I enjoyed the evolution, learning, achievements and interaction of the little ones. I have had much help from many parents, grandparents, children and grandchildren in trying to convey the ideas in this book.

It is hard to tell children that many of their teachers are ignorant activists with no interest in the nation's or children's futures; that their teachers obfuscate and promote disinformation about fundamental science, the environment and history; that they are victims of the left's successful great march through the education system and that a so-called education has not provided children with basic knowledge and the skills to criticise, analyse and argue. It is time to save the children from nonsense. Intelligent knowledgeable people are being silenced such that ignorant stupid people won't be offended.

The author often gets accused of being controversial. If being controversial is to tell the truth, use validated facts and be sceptical of everything, then so be it.

Sources

Alley, N. 2000: The Younger Dryas cold interval as viewed from central Greenland. *Journal of Quaternary Science Reviews* 19, 213-226

Berner, R. A. and Kothavala, Z., 2001: GEOCARB III: A revised model of atmospheric CO_2 over Phanerozoic time. *American Journal of Science* 301, 182-204

https://www.clintel.org An international European-based foundation for climate change and climate policy comprising scientists.

https://www.co2coalition.org The coalition is a non-partisan educational foundation addressing the policy issues of carbon dioxide, climate and science. It is one of the most informative WWW sites on the role of carbon dioxide and climate change. The publish unchallengeable climate facts.

https://www.electroverse.co An outstanding site with a focus on earth changes during the grand solar minimum and space weather with a focus on anomalous cold weather in times of global "boiling".

https://www.ipa.org.au An Australian free market institute that has been a force in politics since 1943. The author is a member and benefactor of the IPA.

http://www.joannenova.com.au One of the most popular and best climate sites in the world. Jo Nova uses logic, science and humour to discuss the latest claims by climate activists, hypocrites and frauds. Essential daily reading.

https://geology.utah.gov/map-pub/survey-notes/glad-you-asked/ice-ages-what-are-they-and-what-causes-them/ This is one of many geological sites that looks back in time at climate change. All have a similar reconstruction of past temperatures and carbon dioxide over time based on ice core drilling, sediment and fossil analysis and proxies.

https://jennifermarahasy.com The site of an Australian biologist who researches the measurement techniques of Australia's Bureau of Meteorology, the Great Barrier Reef and climate. Source of data, films, scientific publications and scientific expertise contrary to that presented by the mainstream media.

https://www.heartland.org A conservative political site that inter alia deals with climate.

Loehle, C. 2007: A 2000-year global temperature reconstruction based on non-tree ring proxies. Energy and Environment 18, 1049-1058

https://www.ncel.NOAA.gov is another source of primary data through NOAA, NASA and the National Centers for Environmental Information. One needs patience to trawl through this site which displays, for example, the global warming in the scale of human temperature experience compared to the magnified warming as presented by the media. This is an absolute essential site for understanding climate.

Petkova, E. P., Gasparrini, A. and Kinney, P. L. 2014: Heat and mortality in New York City since the beginning of the 20th Century. Epidemiology 25(4), 554-560

https://www.prageru.com is a site that finds primary data hidden on official sites and then questions the popular scary narrative presented by the mainstream media and those with a self-interest.

https://public.wmo.int The World Meteorological Organization which is a source of primary data on world death rate from hurricanes, storms and climate, weather-related disasters, global burned areas etc.

Scotese, C. R. 2002: Analysis of the temperature oscillations in geological eras. W. H Freeman and Co., New York

http://www.thegwpf.org A UK-based foundation that deals with the politics and policy of global warming, mainly in the UK but globally. The author sits on the Global Warming Policy Foundation Scientific Advisory Board.

https://www.wattsupwiththat.com is a very popular site of meteorologist Anthony Watts that deals with weather, climate, the latest media exaggerations and analyses official government data. For example, the NOAA average temperature anomaly of the US Climate Reference Network is updated every few weeks, the main stream media never search for the detailed data and sites like WUWT find and publish the data that is contrary to the narrative.

Scientific, philosophical and psychological writings by Alex Epstein, Will Happer, Steven Koonin, Mark Lawson, Nigel Lawson, Richard Lindzen, Christopher Monckton, Patrick Moore, Andrew Montford, Jordan Peterson, Nir Shaviv, Michael Shellenberger, Henrik Svensmark and Valentina Zharkova form the basis of background reading for this book. Activist and blatantly disinformative sites such as Wikipedia, Skeptical science and DeSmog Blog were also visited to keep abreast of the latest scams.

www.ingramcontent.com/pod-product-compliance
Lightning Source LLC
Chambersburg PA
CBHW062012180426
43199CB00034B/2531